Dancing with Presence

Dancing with Presence

Struggling to Grow into Consciousness

by
Don C. Nix, J.D., Ph.D.

iUniverse, Inc.
New York   Bloomington

Dancing with Presence
Struggling to Grow into Consciousness

iUniverse books may be ordered through booksellers or by contacting:

iUniverse
1663 Liberty Drive
Bloomington, IN 47403
www.iuniverse.com
1-800-Authors (1-800-288-4677)

Because of the dynamic nature of the Internet, any Web addresses or links contained in this book
may have changed since publication and may no longer be valid.

ISBN: 978-1-4502-2249-5 (sc)
ISBN: 978-1-4502-2250-1 (ebk)

Printed in the United States of America

iUniverse rev. date: 4/2/2010

Dedication

To my lovely and graceful wife, Ann. The first time I saw you, at seventeen, I thought of a doe, stepping delicately into a sparkling, sunlit stream, and looking out curiously with soft brown eyes at the world and at me. My vision of you has never changed. Now we have shared a life together—shared dreams, shared adventures, shared bodies, shared laughter, shared grief, shared beauty, shared risks, shared pain, shared interests, shared excitements, shared growth, shared family life—almost forty-five years of the roses and thorns that make up a human life. Thank you for choosing me and for being my life/task companion, and thank you for your indulgence, your endurance, and your unique and adventurous spirit. I'll love you forever.

Don C. Nix
Sonoma, CA
April, 2010

Contents

Introduction

The Cosmos is not the dead and empty machine posited by Newton and Descartes. It is sentient and intelligent, every cubit of space and form pulsing with Livingness. Being, the Ocean of Life that throws up and supports the material world, is non-material, beyond our sense perceptions. We can feel It but we can never see It. We can observe Its exquisite handiwork, and sometimes we can perceive Its operations. The main characteristic that is available to our perception is Presence. When our awareness opens and our sensitivity amps up, we can draw near to Being. In those moments, we can feel Its Presence with the cells of the body. It is a distinct and very real experience. It can produce awe and wonder and sometimes boundless gratitude in our hearts. We humans are both innate to this vast Wonder and objectively observing It. We are engaged in a throbbing, drumming, whirling dance with Presence. We call it Life.

1

These are hymns
that I am singing,
in praise
of Power
and Life
and Magic.
These inadequate words
are the only way
that I know
to focus on
the unseeable
Majestic Presence
beneath the world
of form.
In truth,
these words
are just for me,
to wake me up
to Vast Reality.

2

I am Living Space,
temporarily organized
to walk the earth,
and speak my piece,
and play my part,
and unfold my bit
of Boundless Mystery.
My job is to deepen,
to be exactly
who and what I am.
If I decide to hide myself,
the Cosmos will be
incomplete.
In this brief span
that I am here,
I must show up
and play my role.
The Cosmos demands it.

3

My job is
to get out of the way,
to open to Majesty
and carry the cloak.
I am not the doer.
I am along for the ride.
I am temporary help here,
subsumed in Something
so vast and strange
It empties my mind,
as It unfolds Itself
as our world.

4

Who creates?
Not me.
I am only
the fingers of God,
conjured up
for the occasion
by inconceivable
forces of Life.
The impulses
that move through me
are not mine.
They arrive
from above,
and below,
and from every direction
around me.
I am moved,
with compassion,
through the cycle
of my little life.

5

I wanted to be grand
but I didn't know the rules.
In coming here,
I put on separateness
that is all illusion.
If I crave applause
for my separate
little being,
it is because
I have forgotten
the rules of the game.

6

I relax into space.
I release my edges.
I merge with Infinity,
and lose myself
into the Whole,
all without moving
from my chair,
in front of the fire
on this frosty winter
morning.

7

I want to be bigger.
I want to expand my edges.
I want to fly out of
the tiny box
that is me,
and float in
Living Immensity.
It can be done.
I have done it
in the past,
but right now,
in this moment,
it is beyond me.
I am trapped in
myself.

8

It is inexhaustible,
this Mystery that,
from Its profound depths,
throws forth the world.
I touch Its power
and receive Its gifts,
as I take the trouble
to stop myself,
to open myself,
to focus myself
on Unseen Life.
It is always here,
waiting for me,
silent and magnificent.
It is I who
come and go.

9

Presence lies there,
just beyond my reach.
I yearn toward It.
I reach with my mind,
but it is the wrong instrument.
I reach with my cells,
and suddenly
It is here,
intimate and warm
and sublime.
My cells tingle.
My heart opens.
The hair on the
back of my neck
rises.
I soak It in.
My fear vanishes,
and I lose my little self
into Vastness.

10

I reach for my true self,
but it is nowhere to be found.
It is buried,
no doubt,
beneath the strategies
and habits
of this superficial
imposter
that I call me.
I know it is there,
and I know that
it has the answers
for what I should do.
I need these answers,
and I need my true self,
but it is not entirely,
it seems,
up to me.

11

I sit before dawn
in a bubble of peace.
The fire crackles
in the perfect silence.
Another day is coming
to this turbulent,
chaotic world.
So much suffering.
So much glory.
We unfold our story
in a cacophony
of pain,
with moments of bliss
thrown in for
good measure.
It's confusing
and threatening,
this life on Earth,
but I wouldn't have missed
a day of it.

12

I am my own galaxy
of particles and space.
I swirl in place,
pushed by invisible Forces
with invisible motives
that are so vast
that my mind turns off.
I am so small and
That
is so large.
I am so weak and
That
is so strong.
I relax into
my vulnerability,
and realize that
gratitude
is my only option.

13

Things come together
and things come apart,
including me.
Things grow and flourish,
and things wither and die,
including me.
Things have their heyday,
and things become passé,
including me.
The entire Cosmos is
unfolding and changing,
and metamorphosing and passing,
including me.
Don't take it personally.

14

A handful of diamonds
inside my head,
faceted and flashing,
self-luminous,
glinting and glowing
brightly,
as I move through
my day,
magic diamonds
that produce this awareness
that I call me.

15

Disarranged,
disconsolate,
despairing,
I sit in my chair
in the early morning.
I would like
to find my way
back to equilibrium,
but I don't know
in which direction
it lies,
or perhaps I do.
Perhaps it lies
in every direction
around me.
I must turn my cells
outward.
I must stretch
into the space
around me,
seeking Life,
seeking Presence,
seeking the only Thing
that will heal this state.

16

I would like to pull a lever
and go from despair to joy,
but I cannot find it
among the things of my mind.
I am stuck in this tiny box,
my ego mind,
and there is nothing in here
but my problems.
I ring the changes on them
endlessly.
I know that a larger Cosmos
lies waiting outside this box,
an internal shift
that could bring me relief.
But,
for this moment,
I am stuck here,
no lever available,
while I wait for the dawn
to break,
and release me into distraction.

17

How deep can I reach
when my mind is shallow?
How high can I see
when it's all about me?
In this Ocean of Vastness,
I am marooned
in my tiny self.
I wait for daybreak,
or something,
to release me
from this self-made prison
of separateness.

18

What is my through-line?
What is the arc
of my narrative
from here
to the closing chapter?
The past is gone forever.
The future looks dim and bleak.
Loneliness looms ahead,
and fear grips me subtly
and not so subtly.
I know there is a path
out of here,
a path that will refill
my heart
and expand my soul.
But,
for the moment,
I cannot see it.
I cannot reach it.
I must abide
with this experience now.

19

As I write poems
I feel a little better.
My state changes
slowly and subtly.
My spirits rise
as I contemplate
my life and my prospects.
I have a little more hope.
I am forever caught
in this round of states
moving,
like chimera,
through me,
and shifting my experience
from moment to moment.
It's a little exhausting,
and terribly repetitious,
but it is my life,
the only life that I have,
and it gets shorter
with every breath that
I draw.
Try a little gratitude.
Appreciation is the balm
for desolation.

20

I am embedded in a Whole
that has meaning at Its heart.
I am not alone,
but enmeshed in
Mysterious Majesty.
I push outward,
reaching,
eager for the touch
of Vitality
that will enliven me,
and put Its arms around me
forever.

21

I wake from darkness.
My mind lights up,
radiant and reflective,
self-luminous and glowing,
receiving and sending,
a pool of
Unmanifest Livingness.
I rest in Its sensitivity
and connect with the Cosmos.
Another day on Earth.

22

Silence feeds my soul.
I drink it up
into my cells,
like rain into
a dry prairie.
I need it.
I seek it.
I must have it,
if I am ever
to bloom in profusion.

23

I am an observer
on this train,
content with the gift
of watching the scenery go by.
It's an engrossing scene,
and I appreciate
its colors and forms and dramas.
But while it occupies me fully,
this panorama of life,
beneath the excitement
and movement and turbulence,
I sense my awareness
that the final station
lies just up ahead.

24

In an alternate universe,
two and two might be five,
or seven or nine,
or just about any number you wish.
But we are here
in our predictable Cosmos,
where structure and regularity reign.
Where,
beneath the turbulent chaos of our world,
a system of Patterned Order
floats invisible,
in sublime and regal splendor.
I turn toward Its truth,
toward Its dependable habits,
toward Its clarity and radiance and brilliance,
and I am suddenly,
in this moment,
subsumed in Majesty.

25

In due time,
the Universe takes
us apart,
stick by stick by stick,
just as it put
us together,
cell by cell by cell,
and ushered us,
babbling,
into this turbulent world.

26

This pool of
mysterious Consciousness
is not just mine.
This aging, remarkable body
is not just mine.
This life of roses and thorns
is not just mine.
Moment by moment,
I am laced with Grandeur,
and derived from Immensity.
I am along for the ride.
I consent to accept
these wonders,
and play my small bit role
in this production of Splendor.

27

Fear hums in my mind
like the drone of a sitar,
sometimes rising to the surface
and becoming coherent,
sometimes sinking back
to uneasiness
just beneath the surface
of my mind.
How can I neutralize it,
and find my way to joy?
Just keep trying.

28

At seventy-one,
I try to deepen.
I try to widen,
and understand
this turbulent,
chaotic reality.
I try to make use
of this little pool
of miraculous Consciousness,
before I step off
and become the galaxies.

29

I try to open myself.
I try to push my edges
out into the darkness
that is my little world.
I struggle to escape
my confinement,
to become larger
than I can be,
to break through
my smallness.
And sometimes,
who knows why,
it works,
and things change.
The world splits open,
and I break through
into inconceivable Vastness.

30

From separateness,
alone in a hard world,
I look through the surface
of reality.
I touch invisible Being,
and suddenly,
held and warmed,
I am escorted
into Splendor.

31

I am the child of royalty,
born in the Big Bang
and thrown out
by bursting stars
through infinities of night
to become the fecund Earth.
Pushed by Mysterious Forces,
I came from watery depths
out onto the land.
I stood up
and grew my brain larger.
I learned to grow grain,
built cities of stone
and dreams,
and filled the world
with my success.
In time,
I became proud.
I thought I was the Cosmos.
I forgot my Source.
I thought it was me.
Things began to go wrong.
Now, chastened and scared,
I am searching and scanning,
and doing my best
to find my way
back home.

32

I want to be embedded
in the Universe,
with my arms
around the galaxies,
in a reality so intense
that my little self expires.
I want to become
black space,
and bursting stars,
and swinging planets,
and invisible Majesty,
and Vastness beyond compare.

33

I now know
what the program is.
I must lose
my separateness.
I must lose
this misunderstanding
about myself,
and my place
in the scheme of things.
But, I seem to be
attached to it
like a bad habit
from a long time ago.
I must get out
of this little box,
but I will do it later.
Right now,
honestly,
and regrettably,
I must go
and eat my cornflakes.

34

My knowing is stale.
It's knowledge from the past.
In a realm of not knowing,
the world
of wonder
blooms.
Colors intensify.
Forms push forth,
each emerging out
of infinite Mystery,
to become the world
that I live in
and fail
to truly see.

35

This world that I see
is chimera,
conjured and
held together
by Great Mind,
temporary and pulsing,
and emerging constantly
from invisible depths.
Solids are not solid
but tiny bits of Being
held together by
Mystery
that is too deep to see
but not too deep to feel.

36

The space that I see
as empty
is full,
an Ocean of Life
appearing from nowhere
and returning
instantly
back there.
Alive and pulsing
with unexpressed potential,
the Cosmos unfolds itself
before our amazed eyes.
The world is a web of life,
here dense, there sparse,
all fueled by a Mystery
so profound and magnificent
that the stars roar
in approval.

37

I am here
to do Your bidding.
Move me.
Use me.
Flood me with meaning,
and give me
great tasks,
so that I don't fall,
empty and desolate,
back into
my tiny self.
Make me
a bit of Grandeur.
Move me.
Use me.
Now.

38

Fill me
with the electricity
of your Grandeur.
Open my heart
to joy and bliss,
and ecstasies
large and small.
Open my eyes
to Reality,
and fuel my fire
with Depth.
I am waiting,
patiently,
for the touch
of Your unfolding.

39

The media is toxic
to the soul.
Applause empties
the heart of spirit,
and fills it
with smug,
evanescent
self-satisfaction.
Nearness to Being
thrives in solitude.
We must choose
between status
and depth.
It is not even a contest.

40

What is this push
to be seen?
Praise swells
the little self
to great proportions.
Depth disappears.
Smugness is launched,
and,
when the moment passes,
emptiness remains.

41

This theatrical production
has had a good long run,
some good reviews,
a few disgruntled patrons.
It has had its moments
of high drama,
and comedy,
and tenderness,
and tragedy,
and farce.
With a full
and rich heart,
and with gratitude,
I await
the final curtain.

42

Wanting to be seen.
What's that all about?
It's an appetite
derived from emptiness,
that expands
on touch,
continually outstripping
its satisfaction.
It's a siren singing
a false song
to vulnerable little souls
that are yearning,
in truth,
for the touch
of the Cosmos.

43

I sing my praise to Glory.
I dance my dance of offering.
I open myself to Presence,
and I wait to be touched
by Vastness.
I want my head to empty.
I want my heart to open.
I want my nerves to burn
with the fire of
Living Grace.

44

I'm cultivating a rich heart.
I'm not there yet
but I'm on my way.
Each time I turn toward Being,
each time I search for Presence,
each time I touch the Mystery,
I get points in the game.
I'm building richness here,
the ability to receive the gifts
of Living Vastness,
offered freely
to an opening soul.

45

Drown me in Being
today.
Flood me with Presence
today.
Usher me out of myself
and into Living Vastness.
Fill my hungry heart
today.
Expand it beyond its limits.
Pour Grace upon me
and open me
today,
now,
and forever.

46

It's painful to be overlooked.
It feels like denial of worth.
But it's only a misunderstanding
about the source of worth.
I am here now.
I am conscious.
I walk the earth,
a living, astonishing miracle,
for this short time
sustained by Cosmic Life.
Here is my supreme value.
Why would I ever
look elsewhere?

47

Rain falls.
Life deepens.
The fire crackles.
My state changes.
The world alters,
and I am lifted
out of myself,
by wings
I never knew I had.

48

Evidently
I need encouragement
to reach into
my depths.
A hand on the shoulder,
a pat on the back,
a word of praise,
a nod of the head.
I should be able
to stand strong
and alone,
but I find that
that is only an image.
I'm vulnerable to the core,
as I reach for the
Ultimate Hand.

49

I am not the Source.
I emerge,
moment by moment,
from Something greater.
My world comes forth,
moment by moment,
from fecund and
Living Nothingness,
in a ceaseless shower
of benediction.

50

I search for Divinity,
while It is pouring Itself
upon me.
I keep my eyes
tightly shut,
while Radiance pours
through the world.
I find emptiness
where only fullness brims.
The world is overflowing
with Light, and Life
and Magic,
while I look at my toes.
Surely, I can move myself
to a new place,
and open myself to
what is present,
though unseen,
here and now,
and forever.

51

When my heart opens
tears spring to my eyes,
rarely sad,
mostly joy,
at being touched
by Flowing Life.
We understand little
of what we are.
We think that
we can think
our way to
Paradise.
Actually,
it is,
without doubt,
a journey
entirely
of feeling.

52

Throw me in Your river.
Drown me in Your sweetness.
I am a dry desert
waiting for Your rain.
Moisten my parched
and aging heart,
and fly me to
Eternity.

53

I thought You were cold and remote.
I thought I had been overlooked.
I thought I was left all alone here,
and really not up to the task.
Then Something arrived in the room.
I suddenly was not all alone.
Your Presence washed over my grief
and showed me the way
back home.

54

When Presence arrives
no thunderclap sounds,
no brilliant light flashes,
no heavy-browed god
appears in the room.
Just silence,
and deepening,
and shifting sensation.
Perception changes,
and the Reality under reality
emerges,
bearing Its depth
and meaning
and sacredness,
and altering my mind
forevermore.

55

Crafting the poem
is not the point.
It's only a vase
into which I pour
my evanescent
experience,
so that I,
myself,
can see
what miracle
I'm made of.

56

Tonight I'm far from Being,
trapped in my little self.
My mind rings the changes on problems,
and I'm occupied only with me.
I yearn
and I burn
to be greater
than this,
to melt and dissolve
and to blow through my edges,
to find some release
from the box of myself,
to find,
by chance,
the key to the door,
the way into Living Space.

57

Push on into
vague twilight musings.
Continue to wait
for the sun.
Go deep into
Mystery's blankness,
This is the path
I am on.

58

It's an art form
to live with Mystery,
to contemplate
half answers,
obscured,
and to do without proof,
to follow the
deepest stirring
without any
confirmation,
to search for
the Cosmos of Joy,
to find Its
invisible land.

59

If I open myself
and clear myself,
Something may speak
from my depths.
This trivial me,
and my trivial mind
may vanish in Cosmic Life.
Then truth might come
and depth might come,
and I might touch the Ultimate One.
But, clearing my mind
seems beyond me.
My mind is full of clutter.
I can see from this place,
this place where I stand,
that my mind keeps me
from my Source.

60

I need to lose my edges
and become the vast blue sky.
I need to soar in tandem,
and find myself
with swirling planets
and exploding stars.
I need to reach into Vastness.
and roam in realms of delight,
I'm greater than this little me,
and I can learn to fly.

61

On the edge of sleep
my mind empties,
my mind drifts.
I wait
for the arrival
of Something
to carry me
out of myself,
Something to free me
from this tight little box
where I'm condemned
to live my life.
I want to fly out
of restriction,
and soar in realms above.
But, for the moment
I'm stuck here,
my little self
in my little bed,
waiting.

62

The earth moves
and death strikes.
Pluto arrives
from the Netherworld.
Our dreams of controlling
our lives are smashed.
We emerge
in all our frailty.
We remember then
our smallness.
We are transient here
and vulnerable.
Our arrogance disappears.
Surely,
it's a high price to pay
to be reminded
of the implacable,
cataclysmic side
of the Force
out of which we spring.

63

Creativity is nothing but
Being's flow
through Its shimmering creation.
Restless and turbulent,
Life moves through
the world,
metamorphosing Itself
eternally.
We live in this maelstrom
of change,
where the old
is continually taken apart
to make way for
the fresh and the new,
including,
someday soon,
this little being
called me.

64

From the Cosmos I came.
In the Cosmos I grew,
not haphazardly,
but according to
profound and ancient patterns,
buried so deeply in Being
that the stars
could not shine
without them.
We're in the hands
of an exquisite Artisan
whose works are sublime
all around us.
We live in this
realm of Splendor,
and look only
at our toes.

65

I yearn to burst
my boundaries.
I want to be bigger
than this.
I want to roar
with the suns,
and swing with
the swirling moons.
I want to touch
Living Light,
and Radiant Blackness too.
I want to dissolve
into space,
and float in
worlds of wonder.

66

My yearning never ceases.
I am intrinsically incomplete.
I am separated from
the Beloved,
though Its everywhere
all around me.
In moments
the prison walls open,
and I touch the electric Source.
My agony turns to wonder
And I wake,
disappeared and complete.

67

The epiphany arrives,
Zeus appears,
not as a grandiose human,
but in his true form
as silent, boundless Space,
as a billion, billion galaxies
foaming with potential life,
as a billion, billion stars
sending their
radiance and life
out into the Living Darkness,
as billions and billions of humans,
dreaming their dreams,
and plotting their plots,
and fearing their fears,
and pushing their chaotic way
into a distant and
uncertain future.

68

It is evident,
if one looks at it,
that the earth itself
is in spasm,
engorged with
Cosmic forces
of death and rebirth,
of destruction and re-creation.
Not for a moment
do I believe
that we are being punished.
The earth could,
if it wished,
in an instant,
throw us completely away.
This is just a response
to juvenile unconsciousness,
a reminder to please,
beginning now,
care for our parent/home.

69

It begins to come clear,
the form it will take,
this smashing of old
and creation of new.
The earth will heave.
The seas will rise.
The heavens will fall
in murderous fire.
We will be taught
to give our attention
to First Things first
and First Things last.
Those who survive
will find a new world,
all scathed and shriven,
all chastened and humbled,
all ready and searching
for a deeper, richer Mind.

70

I am a flow of Being.
From nothing
I have been made
into something.
Each breath that I draw
is a sigh of the world.
Each thought that I think
is a bursting of Light.
I move among patterns
of beauty and grace,
unfolding the Source
in my own little way.
I move in the web
of the Life-Force,
with thunder of
galaxies distantly heard.
I walk the earth.
I think,
I live.
I am graced.

71

Words tumble.
Thoughts flare.
Worlds turn.
Moons swing.
The Cosmos is dancing
Its stately dance,
as I lie in my bed
awake,
alive to the drama,
the stately pavane,
to music I make
in my head.

72

What magic is this
that the rhythm of words
sets off swirling of worlds
in my head?
Galaxies crash
and suns explode,
and great waves rock
The Cosmos
while I lie in bed.
I open myself,
I leap out of myself,
I expand myself
to get the view.
I relish this sport.
I relish this life.
I'm a spectator
of Magnificence.

73

It takes a trillion
processes per second
to keep me on this earth,
each essential and coherent
and woven with artistry
into the web of my life.
Am I important?
I'm more than that.
I'm vital
to the Cosmos.
The proof is that
I'm here
on Earth,
on center stage,
singing my aria.

74

I dance my Dance
of the Seven Fans,
letting just bits
of myself be seen.
I'm a constellation
of planets,
and stars,
and moons,
dancing and shifting
their shape,
an arrangement of
ordered nuance,
driven by internal fires
held deep in
Primordial Life.

75

I may not be big
but I'm grand.
My design is of the best.
My parts fit all together,
hosted by Mystery,
moving through cycles,
going I know not where
for reasons I know not why.
What a ride!

76

I'm walking the earth
as I speak,
Every step a miracle
of bones,
and blood,
and sinews,
and thought,
and breath.
and Life.
I am a symphony walking,
a complexity in motion.
I am the latest model
of this fabulous, mysterious animal,
designed and unfolded
through eons,
and walking,
here and now,
through the Cosmos.

77

I'm crying with joy
in the night.
My heart is spilling over.
This means that
I'm still alive.
My heart is still moist,
and softened and rich,
and full of
the sweetness of Being.
I am blessed by Mystery now
as I open myself to the world.